The Author's Photograph Collection
By Steve Presley

Here are some pictures of me: Most are about Peru, Indiana and at the Oak Haven
Stables on State Hwy 31 seven miles southwest of town. The big black and white horse
is my horse, Marshal Dillon. He is Belgian/Clydesdale draft horse mixed with Tennessee
walking horse. I have his mother's blood line back to the year 1125. He is related to the
Pusher C.G., Seabiscuit, and Trigger Jr. The cars are a 1988 Chevrolet S-10, a 2003
Buick Century, an 2000 Jaguar Type S, and a 1086 Corvette fastback.

Pictures of me:

Pictures of my home:

Pictures of me and my horse, Marshal Dillon:

Pictures of me and my cars:

Pictures of me hunting:

The End

www.ingramcontent.com/pod-product-compliance
Lightning Source LLC
Chambersburg PA
CBHW080525190526
45169CB00008B/3060